# the BAND book

### How many silly, funky, crazy bands do you own?

by Ilanit Oliver
illustrated by Dan Potash

Simon Spotlight
New York   London   Toronto   Sydney

# the BAND book

## How many silly, funky, crazy bands do you own?

SIMON SPOTLIGHT
An imprint of Simon & Schuster Children's Publishing Division
1230 Avenue of the Americas, New York, New York 10020
© 2010 by Simon & Schuster, Inc.
All rights reserved, including the right of reproduction in whole or in
part in any form. SIMON SPOTLIGHT and colophon are registered
trademarks of Simon & Schuster, Inc. For information about special
discounts for bulk purchases, please contact Simon & Schuster
Special Sales at 1-866-506-1949 or business@simonandschuster.com.
Manufactured in the United States of America 0710 CWM
First Edition 10 9 8 7 6 5 4 3 2 1
ISBN 978-1-4424-2027-4

Front cover (locker and padlock image) photograph © 2010 Getty
Images; Front cover (hand image) photograph by Dan Potash; Back
cover photograph © 2010 Getty Images; Page 6-7 photograph ©
2010 Getty Images; Page 8-9 photograph © 2010 iStockphoto; Page
12-13 photograph © 2010 Jetta Productions; Page 14-15 photograph
© 2010 iStockphoto; Page 18-19 photograph © 2010 Getty Images;
Page 20-21 photograph © 2010 iStockphoto; Page 22-23 photograph
© 2010 Hemera; Page 26 photograph © 2010 iStockphoto; Page
28-29 photograph © 2010 Comstock; Page 30 photograph © 2010
Ryan McVay; Page 34-35 photograph © 2010 iStockphoto; Page 36
photograph © 2010 Getty Images; Page 38-39 photograph © 2010
Medioimages/Photodisc; Page 42-43 photograph © 2010 iStockphoto;
Page 44-45 photograph © 2010 Medioimages/Photodisc; Page 48-
49 photograph © 2010 Mike Powell; Page 52-53 photograph © 2010
Jetta Productions; Page 56 photograph © 2010 Hemera; Page 61
photograph © 2010 Getty Images; Page 64-65 photograph © 2010
Thinkstock; Page 70-71 photograph © 2010 Getty Images; Page 74
photograph © 2010 Getty Images; Page 76-77 photograph © 2010
iStockphoto; Page 96 photograph © 2010 Siri Stafford

It's time to get silly.

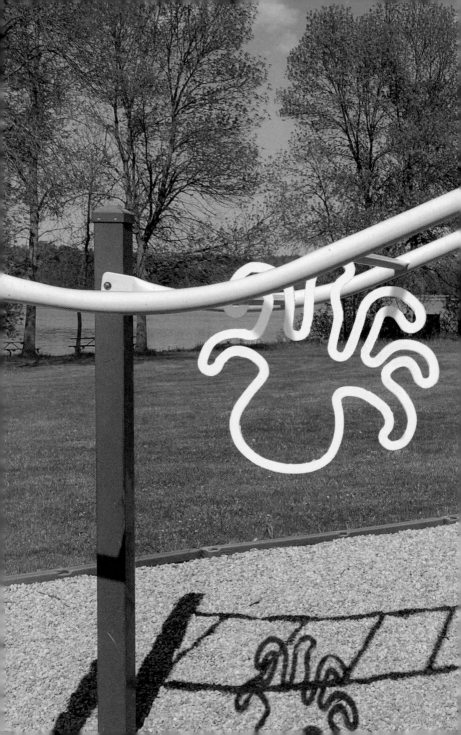

# !!! The Ultimate BAND QUIZ !!!

**#1** how many bands do you own?

- ☐ less than 20
- ☐ 20 - 50
- ☐ 50 - 100
- ☐ 100 - 200
- ☐ 200 - 300
- ☐ more than 300!

#2

what's your
**FAVORITE**
band?

#3

what's the

## RAREST

band you have

**#6**

have you ever
photographed
glow = in - the - dark
bands with the
lights
OFF?

#7

if the **Giraffe** band

and the **Octopus** band

had a baby,

what would it

look like ???

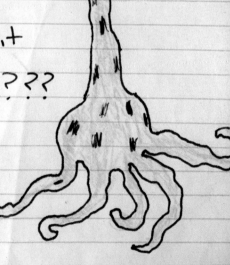

**#8**

if you were a band

which

# BAND

would you be

heghog ?

nice bubble letters!

danny says my bubble letters are lame!

#9

how many bands would  **YOU TRADE** for a

really rare one (like a phoenix, white ghost, or three-headed dragon )

☐ 1           ☐ 10-15

☐ 2 - 5      ☑ 16-20

☐ 6 -10      ☐ 21-25

**?**

how many bands

are you wearing

# RIGHT
# NOW?

#10

#11

which wrestling team

would you

# WANT

to see in the

# RING ?

( check only ONE! )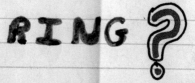

that means you, Chris!

☐ LEPRECHAUN VS. GENIE

☑ MERMAID VS. TWO-HEADED DRAGON

☐ CATERPILLAR VS. SNAIL

☐ EASTER BUNNY VS. LOBSTER

**#12**

# TO LEND
## or
# NOT TO LEND
## ?

"I would <u>NEVER</u> <u>EVER</u>

<u>EVER</u> lend my bands to..."

☐ friends      ☐ parents

☐ siblings      ☐ crushes

#14

how **BIG**

do you want

your band collection

**GET** to **?**

- ☑ 100 - 200
- ☐ 200 - 400
- ☐ 500 - 1000
- ☐ 1000 - 1500
- ☐ 1500 - 2500
- ☐ 5000 and up!

# do you ever take your bands OFF?

yes!
but
i would want
to keep them
on, but there a
little ichy

#16

in your group
of friends,
who has the
BIGGEST
band collection

1. _____

2. _____

3. _____

4. _____

5. _____

6. _____

7. _____

8. _____

9. _____

10. _____

#17

what are the

TOP 10

most popular

bands in school

? ? ?

1. _____
2. _____
3. _____
4. _____
5. _____
6. _____
7. _____
8. _____
9. _____
10. _____

#19

what would you do
to get **bands**
allowed back in school **?**

☐ extra homework
☐ help the lunchroom staff serve
☐ wash dirty towels after gym class
☐ clip the principal's toenails
☐ all of the above!
☐ none of the above!

#20

do you have

a

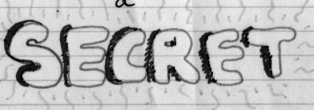
SECRET

hiding place

for your

bands?

which band do you think would be most likely to be sent

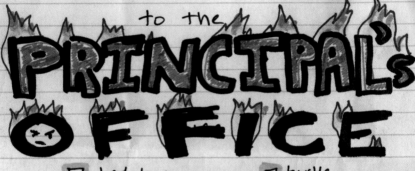

to the PRINCIPAL's OFFICE

☐ ladybug          ☐ turtle

☐ dolphin          ☐ lamb

☐ starfish

what was the very

## VERY
## VERY

first band you ever

got **?**

# DiD you...

☐ buy it **?**

☐ steal it from your brother **?**

☐ trade your turkey sandwich for it **?**

☐ do a certain someone's history homework ALL week long AND explain every detail to them for what seemed like hours ... **?**

#23

what was the

most recent

# BAND

you got ?

?

#24

who was the **FIRST** one of your friends to wear **BANDS** ?

if it was your

# job

to pick the

# theme

for a  new  pack  of  bands,

what  would  you  pick?

**#26**

do you have

enough bands to...

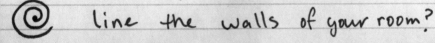
cover your **WHOLE** bed?

line the walls of your room?

**FILL** your bathtub?

#27

HAVE YOU

EVER COVERED

YOUR

# ENTIRE

ARM WITH

BANDs

?

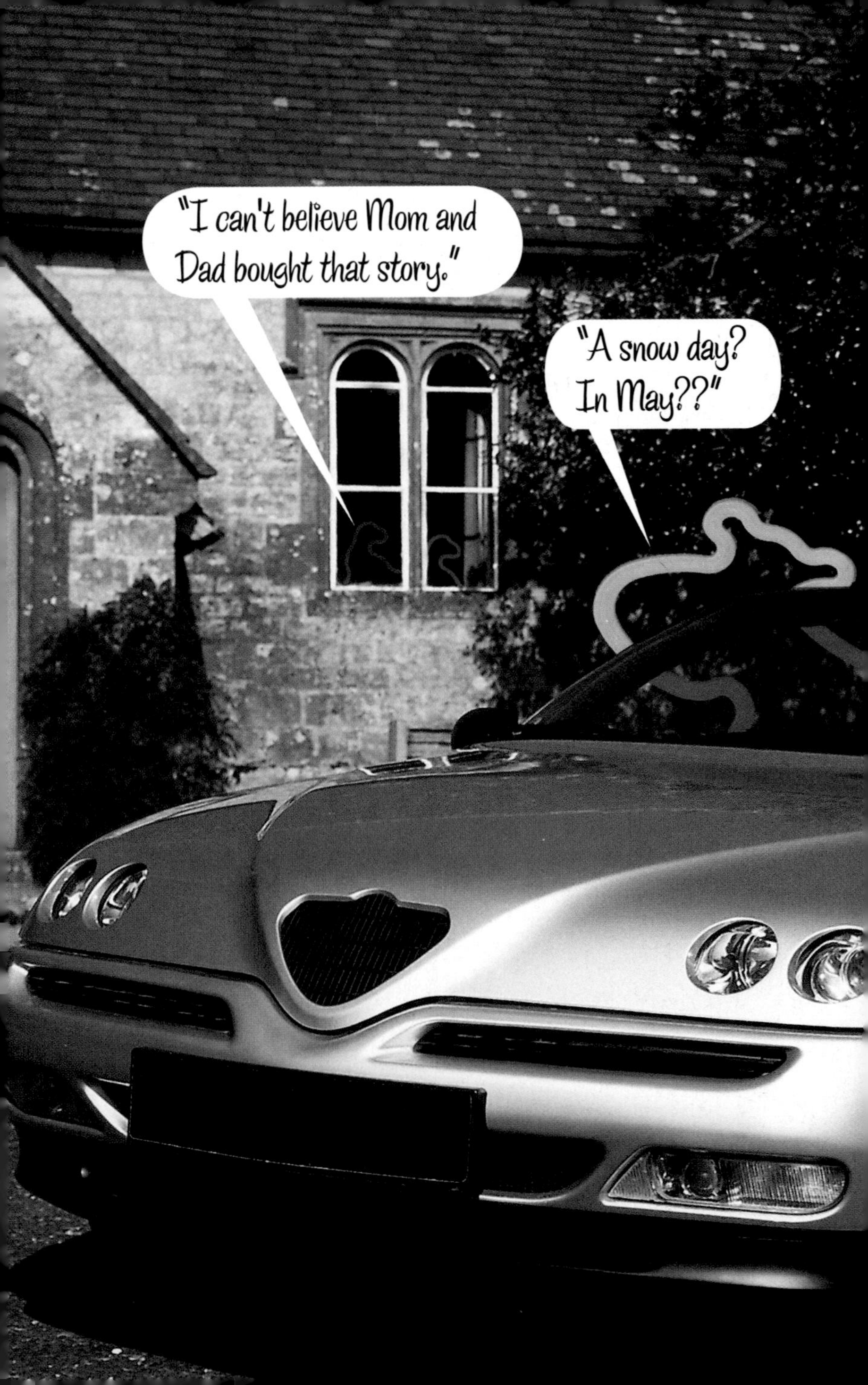
"I can't believe Mom and Dad bought that story."
"A snow day? In May??"

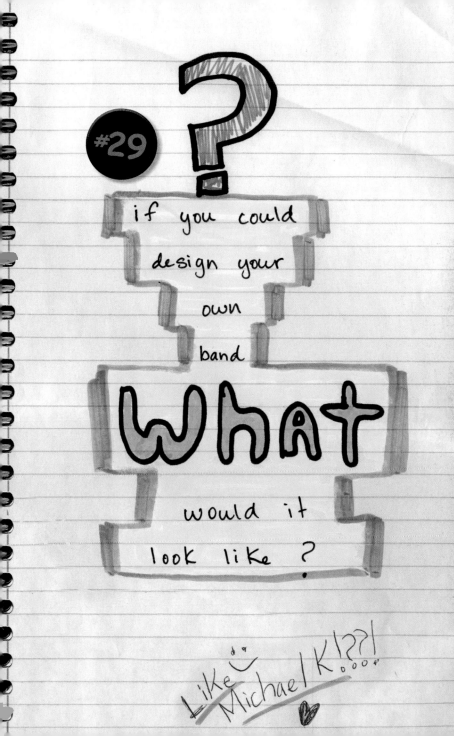

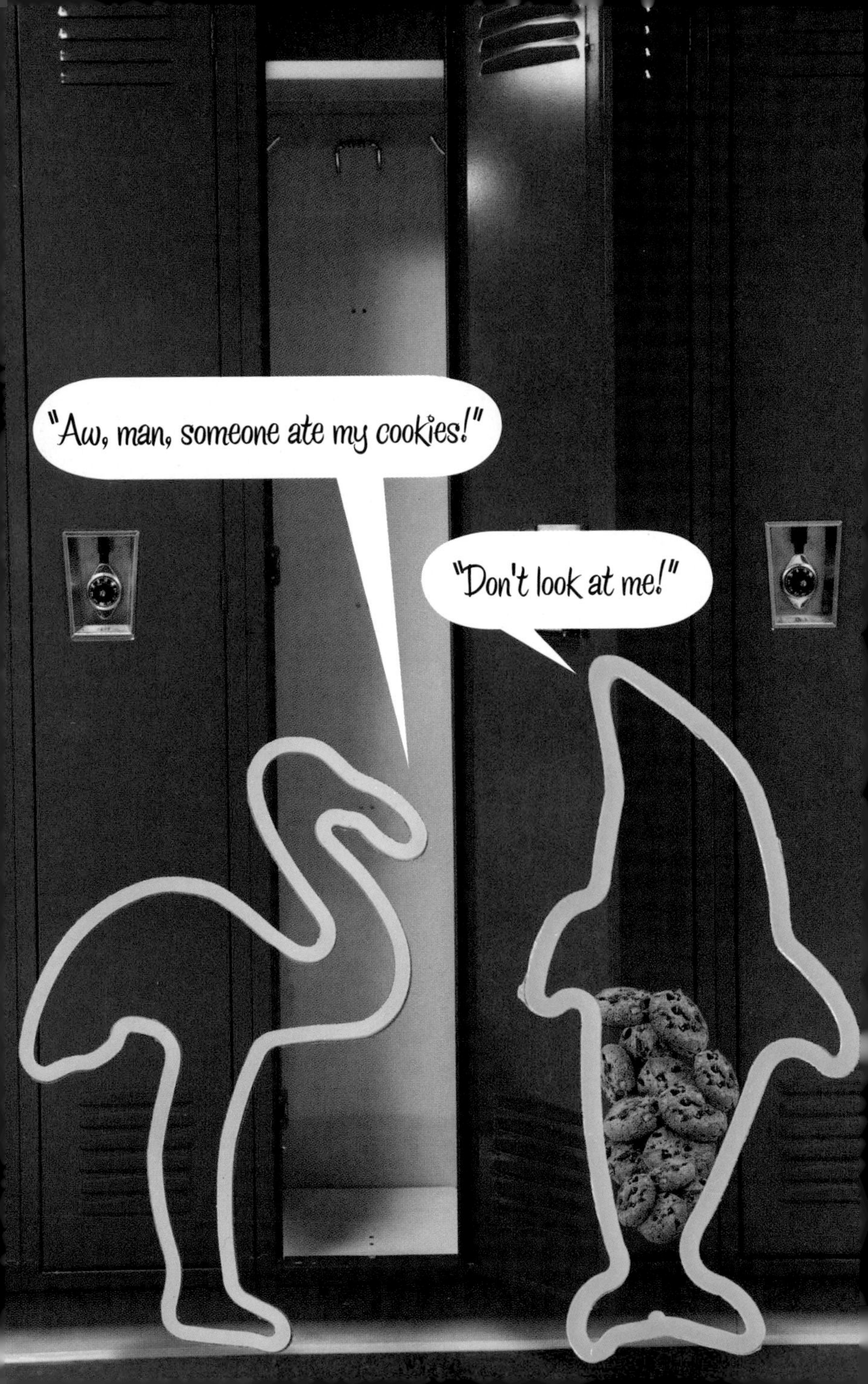
"Aw, man, someone ate my cookies!"
"Don't look at me!"

# MATCH

**#30**

the bands

below

to your closest

# FRIENDs

the two-headed dragon is _____

the baseball cap is _____

the butterfly is _____

the phoenix is _____

the werewolf is _____

the skull and crossbones are _____

and _____

# Band Check List

Got 'em all? Check 'em off!

## Icons

- ☑ Girl
- ☐ Star
- ☐ Money Sign
- ☑ Bone
- ☐ Heart
- ☐ Moon
- ☐ Sun
- ☐ Peace Sign
- ☐ _____
- ☐ _____

# Sports

- ☐ Baseball
- ☑ Hockey Stick
- ☑ Tennis Racket
- ☐ Baseball Cap
- ☐ Base Plate
- ☐ Skate
- ☐ Baseball Pitcher
- ☐ Baseball Batter
- ☐ Football Helmet
- ☐ Megaphone
- ☐ Football
- ☐ Mascots
- ☐ Basketball
- ☐ Jersey

- ☐ Baseball Bat
- ☐ Baseball Cleats
- ☐ Baseball Glove
- ☐ Golf Bag
- ☐ _____
- ☐ _____
- ☐ _____
- ☐ _____
- ☐ _____
- ☐ _____
- ☐ _____
- ☐ _____
- ☐ _____
- ☐ _____

# Wild Animals

- [ ] Lion
- [ ] Bear
- [x] Giraffe
- [x] Elephant
- [x] Hippo
- [x] Rhino
- [ ] Wolf
- [x] Kangaroo
- [ ] Flamingo
- [ ] Gecko
- [ ] Tree Frog
- [ ] Panther
- [ ] Gorilla
- [ ] Monkey
- [ ] Camel

- [ ] Boar
- [ ] Raccoon
- [ ] _echie_
- [ ] _____
- [ ] _____
- [ ] _____
- [ ] _____
- [ ] _____
- [ ] _____
- [ ] _____
- [ ] _____
- [ ] _____
- [ ] _____
- [ ] _____
- [ ] _____

# Farm Animals

- ☑ Pig
- ☐ Owl
- ☐ Horse
- ☑ Rooster
- ☐ Goat
- ☐ _____
- ☐ _____
- ☐ _____
- ☐ _____
- ☐ _____
- ☐ _____
- ☐ _____
- ☐ _____
- ☐ _____
- ☐ _____

- ☐ _____
- ☐ _____
- ☐ _____
- ☐ _____
- ☐ _____
- ☐ _____
- ☐ _____
- ☐ _____
- ☐ _____
- ☐ _____
- ☐ _____
- ☐ _____
- ☐ _____
- ☐ _____
- ☐ _____

# Birds and Insects

- ☐ Caterpillar
- ☐ Spider
- ☐ Butterfly
- ☐ Ladybug
- ☐ Snail
- ☐ Bumblebee
- ☐ Hummingbird
- ☑ Parrot
- ☐ Dove
- ☐ Toucan
- ☑ spider
- ☑ centipeed
- ☐ _____
- ☐ _____
- ☐ _____

- ☐ _____
- ☐ _____
- ☐ _____
- ☐ _____
- ☐ _____
- ☐ _____
- ☐ _____
- ☐ _____
- ☐ _____
- ☐ _____
- ☐ _____
- ☐ _____
- ☐ _____
- ☐ _____
- ☐ _____

# Fantasy

- [ ] Dragons
- [x] Mermaids
- [x] Fairies
- [ ] Unicorn
- [ ] Castle
- [ ] Princess
- [ ] Genie
- [ ] Genie's Lamp
- [ ] Phoenix
- [ ] Leprechaun
- [ ] 2-Headed Dragon
- [ ] Vampire Fangs
- [ ] Rose
- [ ] Werewolf
- [ ] _____

- [ ] _____
- [ ] _____
- [ ] _____
- [ ] _____
- [ ] _____
- [ ] _____
- [ ] _____
- [ ] _____
- [ ] _____
- [ ] _____
- [ ] _____
- [ ] _____
- [ ] _____
- [ ] _____
- [ ] _____

# Dinosaurs

- ☐ T-Rex
- ☐ Brontosaurus
- ☐ Triceratops
- ☐ Stegosaurus
- ☐ Velociraptor
- ☐ Dilophosaurus
- ☐ Dinosaur Footprint
- ☐ _____
- ☐ _____
- ☐ _____
- ☐ _____
- ☐ _____
- ☐ _____
- ☐ _____
- ☐ _____

- ☐ _____
- ☐ _____
- ☐ _____
- ☐ _____
- ☐ _____
- ☐ _____
- ☐ _____
- ☐ _____
- ☐ _____
- ☐ _____
- ☐ _____
- ☐ _____
- ☐ _____
- ☐ _____
- ☐ _____

# Pirates and Vikings

- ☐ Viking
- ☐ Viking Shield
- ☐ Viking Helmet
- ☐ Battle Axe
- ☐ Ship
- ☐ Sword
- ☐ Pirate
- ☐ Skull and Crossbones
- ☐ Parrot
- ☐ Anchor
- ☐ _____
- ☐ _____
- ☐ _____
- ☐ _____
- ☐ _____

- ☐ _____
- ☐ _____
- ☐ _____
- ☐ _____
- ☐ _____
- ☐ _____
- ☐ _____
- ☐ _____
- ☐ _____
- ☐ _____
- ☐ _____
- ☐ _____
- ☐ _____
- ☐ _____
- ☐ _____

# Holiday

- ☐ Christmas Tree
- ☐ Easter Bunny
- ☐ Angel
- ☐ Candy Cane
- ☐ Snowman
- ☐ Stocking
- ☑ ghost
- ☑ spider
- ☑ bat
- ☑ witch
- ☑ zombie
- ☑ pumpkin
- ☐ _____
- ☐ _____
- ☐ _____

- ☐ _____
- ☐ _____
- ☐ _____
- ☐ _____
- ☐ _____
- ☐ _____
- ☐ _____
- ☐ _____
- ☐ _____
- ☐ _____
- ☐ _____
- ☐ _____
- ☐ _____
- ☐ _____
- ☐ _____

# Pets

- [x] Dog
- [x] Cat
- [x] Turtle
- [x] Bird
- [x] Rabbit
- [ ] _____
- [ ] _____
- [ ] _____
- [ ] _____
- [ ] _____
- [ ] _____
- [ ] _____
- [ ] _____
- [ ] _____
- [ ] _____

- [ ] _____
- [ ] _____
- [ ] _____
- [ ] _____
- [ ] _____
- [ ] _____
- [ ] _____
- [ ] _____
- [ ] _____
- [ ] _____
- [ ] _____
- [ ] _____
- [ ] _____
- [ ] _____
- [ ] _____

# Sea Creatures

- [x] Dolphin
- [x] Fish
- [x] Seahorse
- [ ] Lobster
- [ ] Starfish
- [x] Shark
- [x] Seals
- [x] Penguin
- [ ] Alligator
- [ ] Stingray
- [ ] _____
- [ ] _____
- [ ] _____
- [ ] _____
- [ ] _____

- [ ] _____
- [ ] _____
- [ ] _____
- [ ] _____
- [ ] _____
- [ ] _____
- [ ] _____
- [ ] _____
- [ ] _____
- [ ] _____
- [ ] _____
- [ ] _____
- [ ] _____

# Spring

- [ ] Flowers
- [x] Duck
- [x] Dragonfly
- [ ] Lamb
- [ ] Butterfly
- [ ] Kite
- [ ] Chick
- [ ] Egg
- [ ] _____
- [ ] _____
- [ ] _____
- [ ] _____
- [ ] _____
- [ ] _____
- [ ] _____

- [ ] _____
- [ ] _____
- [ ] _____
- [ ] _____
- [ ] _____
- [ ] _____
- [ ] _____
- [ ] _____
- [ ] _____
- [ ] _____
- [ ] _____
- [ ] _____
- [ ] _____
- [ ] _____
- [ ] _____

# Western

- ☐ Cowboy Boots
- ☐ Cowboy Hat
- ☐ Sheriff Badge
- ☐ Horse
- ☐ Cactus
- ☐ Horseshoe
- ☐ Longhorn Skull
- ☐ Coyote
- ☐ _____
- ☐ _____
- ☐ _____
- ☐ _____
- ☐ _____
- ☐ _____
- ☐ _____

- ☐ _____
- ☐ _____
- ☐ _____
- ☐ _____
- ☐ _____
- ☐ _____
- ☐ _____
- ☐ _____
- ☐ _____
- ☐ _____
- ☐ _____
- ☐ _____
- ☐ _____
- ☐ _____
- ☐ _____

## Music

- [x] Guitar
- [ ] Rock Hand
- [x] Microphone Stand
- [x] Drums
- [ ] Jumping Rocker
- [ ] Saxophone
- [ ] Electric Guitar
- [ ] Music Notes
- [x] trumpet
- [x] villolin
- [ ] _____
- [ ] _____
- [ ] _____
- [ ] _____
- [ ] _____

- [ ] _____
- [ ] _____
- [ ] _____
- [ ] _____
- [ ] _____
- [ ] _____
- [ ] _____
- [ ] _____
- [ ] _____
- [ ] _____
- [ ] _____
- [ ] _____
- [ ] _____
- [ ] _____
- [ ] _____

# Beach Theme

- ☐ Sand Castle
- ☐ Seashell
- ☐ Wave
- ☐ Surfboard
- ☐ Palm Tree
- ☐ Bathing Suit
- ☐ Suntan Lotion
- ☐ Bikini
- ☐ Sunglasses
- ☐ Shovel
- ☐ Crab
- ☐ Beach Umbrella
- ☐ Lifeguard Stand
  with Umbrella
- ☐ Swim Trunks

- ☐ Sun
- ☐ Lounge Chair
- ☐ _____
- ☐ _____
- ☐ _____
- ☐ _____
- ☐ _____
- ☐ _____
- ☐ _____
- ☐ _____
- ☐ _____
- ☐ _____
- ☐ _____
- ☐ _____
- ☐ _____

## Girly

- ☐ Tiara
- ☐ Diamond Ring
- ☐ Glass Slipper
- ☐ Magic Wand
- ☑ Lips
- ☐ High-Heeled Boot
- ☐ Poodle
- ☑ Lipstick
- ☐ Girl in Fancy Dress
- ☐ Hair Dryer
- ☐ Purse
- ☐ Perfume Bottle
- ☐ Nail Polish Bottle
- ☐ Hairbrush
- ☐ Limousine

- ☐ _____
- ☐ _____
- ☐ _____
- ☐ _____
- ☐ _____
- ☐ _____
- ☐ _____
- ☐ _____
- ☐ _____
- ☐ _____
- ☐ _____
- ☐ _____
- ☐ _____
- ☐ _____
- ☐ _____

# Food

- ☐ Ice-Cream Cone
- ☐ Ring Pop
- ☐ Lollipop
- ☐ Gummy Bear
- ☐ Hard Candy
- ☐ Carrot
- ☐ Hot Dog
- ☐ Hamburger
- ☐ French Fries
- ☐ Pizza
- ☐ Drink Cup
- ☐ _____
- ☐ _____
- ☐ _____
- ☐ _____

- ☐ _____
- ☐ _____
- ☐ _____
- ☐ _____
- ☐ _____
- ☐ _____
- ☐ _____
- ☐ _____
- ☐ _____
- ☐ _____
- ☐ _____
- ☐ _____
- ☐ _____
- ☐ _____
- ☐ _____

## ABC and 123

- ☐ Alphabet
- ☐ Numbers

## Got more? List 'em here!

| | |
|---|---|
| ☐ _____ | ☐ _____ |
| ☐ _____ | ☐ _____ |
| ☐ _____ | ☐ _____ |
| ☐ _____ | ☐ _____ |
| ☐ _____ | ☐ _____ |
| ☐ _____ | ☐ _____ |
| ☐ _____ | ☐ _____ |
| ☐ _____ | ☐ _____ |
| ☐ _____ | ☐ _____ |